i love Birds

Barbara Miller

Book design copyright © 2016
Cover and interior design by Cecille Kaye Gumadan
Illustrations by Kenneth rede Rikimaru

Published in the United States of America

ISBN: 9780692991992
Juvenile Nonfiction / Animals / Birds
15.10.30

For my grandchildren:

Katy, Alexander, Max, Spencer, and Parker

And all children everywhere who are

interested in birds.

Some birds are **big**.

Some birds are **small**...

Hummingbirds are our smallest birds.

Hummingbirds have long, thin bills for sipping food from flowers.

Goldfinches are tiny
yellow birds.
Goldfinches have black wings.

Chickadee is small and gray
and white.
Chickadee's cap is black.

Bluebirds eat worms.

Bluebirds build their nests

in boxes.

Cardinals are pretty red birds.

Robins have red breasts.

Robins sing a cheerful song.

Mockingbirds are mostly gray. White patches show on wings and long tail when they fly. **Mockingbirds** sing other birds' songs.

Woodpeckers peck wood,

looking for food.

Crows are black.

Crows say, "Caw! Caw!"

Owls fly at night.

Owls say, "Who, whoo!"

Ducks swim.

Ducks say, "Quack, quack!"

Gulls are beach birds.

The **bald eagle** is big and strong.
The bald eagle flies so high.
The **bald eagle** is black with a white
head and a white tail.
The **bald eagle** is our national bird.

Some birds are big.
Some birds are small.

I love them all!

NAME the BIRDS!

NAME the BIRDS!

_____